SPEED MACHINES

SNOWMOBILES

BY MATT SCHEFF

SportsZone

An Imprint of Abdo Publishing
www.abdopublishing.com

www.abdopublishing.com

Published by Abdo Publishing, a division of ABDO, PO Box 398166, Minneapolis, Minnesota 55439. Copyright © 2015 by Abdo Consulting Group, Inc. International copyrights reserved in all countries. No part of this book may be reproduced in any form without written permission from the publisher. SportsZone™ is a trademark and logo of Abdo Publishing.

Printed in the United States of America, North Mankato, Minnesota
092014
012015

Cover Photo: Marcel Jancovic/Shutterstock Image
Interior Photos: Marcel Jancovic/Shutterstock Images, 1, 22-23, 26-27, 28-29, 31; Nathan Bilow/AP Images, 4-5, 6-7, 7; National Postal Museum/Curatorial Photographic Collection, 8-9; Bettmann/Corbis, 10-11; Glen Gaffney/Shutterstock Images, 12-13, 20-21; Shutterstock Images, 14-15, 18-19, 24-25; Dmitri Melnik/Shutterstock Images, 15; Carolina K. Smith MD/Shutterstock Images, 16-17; Mark Bonham/Shutterstock Images, 19

Editor: Chrös McDougall
Series Designer: Nikki Farinella

Library of Congress Control Number: 2014944190

Cataloging-in-Publication Data
Scheff, Matt.
 Snowmobiles / Matt Scheff.
   p. cm. -- (Speed machines)
ISBN 978-1-62403-613-2 (lib. bdg.)
Includes bibliographical references and index.
1. Snowmobiles--Juvenile literature.   I. Title.
629.22--dc23

                                                       2014944190

CONTENTS

TAKING THE LEAD

Fifteen snowmobile engines roar as the 2013 Winter X Games snocross final begins. The racers battle for position as the machines soar over huge jumps. One racer loses control and veers off course. All eyes are on the No. 68 Arctic Cat driven by Tucker Hibbert. Hibbert has won the gold medal each of the last five years.

Tucker Hibbert races to the front at the start of a snocross race.

Tucker Hibbert flies through the air during a snocross race.

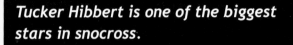

Tucker Hibbert is one of the biggest stars in snocross.

THE HISTORY OF SNOWMOBILES

In 1913, automobile sales in the United States were booming. But the vehicles were not yet able to drive over snow. Car dealer Virgil White wanted to change that. He modified a Ford Model T. He replaced the back wheels with a track. Instead of front wheels, he put skis. It was the first snowmobile.

FAST FACT

In 1922, 15-year-old Joseph-Armand Bombardier of Canada built his own snowmobile. Bombardier went on to start Ski-Doo.

A man stands next to a Ford Model T that was made into a crude snowmobile.

People loved the idea of driving over snow. But most early models were just modified cars. The modern snowmobile didn't exist until 1956. David Johnson worked for Polaris, a company that made farm equipment. In his spare time, Johnson helped build the first modern snowmobile.

FAST FACT

Johnson's bosses at Polaris didn't like his snowmobile at first. But when a customer bought it, they changed their minds.

Former Green Bay Packers quarterback Bart Starr rides a snowmobile in 1968.

Modern snowmobiles are powerful driving machines.

Snowmobiles have come a long way since then. As technology improved, the engines became smaller yet more powerful. Builders also gave the machines better suspension systems. The suspension systems helped the machines sail over bumpy snow and ice. In addition, the popularity of snowmobile racing has led to ultra-high-performance racing sleds.

FAST FACT

In 1968, Ralph Plaisted of Minnesota went to the North Pole on a snowmobile. It was the first motorized vehicle ever to go there.

SNOWMOBILE DESIGN

Snowmobiles have wheels but no tires. A series of small wheels in the back of a sled turn a flexible belt called a track. The track has sharp ridges or metal studs on the outside. These studs dig into the snow and push the sled forward. The front of a snowmobile has a pair of skis. The skis glide over the snow just like a pair of ordinary snow skis. The skis also help steer the snowmobile.

A snowmobile cruises through a snowy forest.

A snowmobile track

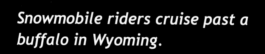

Snowmobile riders cruise past a buffalo in Wyoming.

The metal frame of a snowmobile is called the chassis. All of the other parts connect to the chassis. These parts include the handlebars, body panels, and suspension system. The body panels are made of a strong, lightweight material, such as plastic or carbon fiber. They are shaped to cut through the air with little resistance.

A rider goes airborne on a snowmobile.

Engines give snowmobiles their power. They are measured in cubic centimeters (cc). The bigger the engine, the more powerful it is. High-powered racing sleds can have engines up to 1200cc.

Some snowmobiles are designed for kids. They should only be driven with adult supervision. They have

A rider cuts through powder.

FAST FACT

The fastest sleds can race over snow at 100 miles per hour (161 km/h), or more!

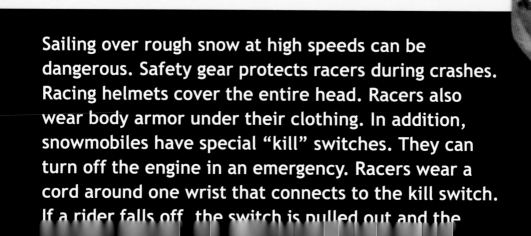

Sailing over rough snow at high speeds can be dangerous. Safety gear protects racers during crashes. Racing helmets cover the entire head. Racers also wear body armor under their clothing. In addition, snowmobiles have special "kill" switches. They can turn off the engine in an emergency. Racers wear a cord around one wrist that connects to the kill switch. If a rider falls off, the switch is pulled out and the

Safety equipment is important both for racing and recreational snowmobiling.

PHOTO DIAGRAM

1. Handlebars

2. Windshield

3. Body

4. Track

5. Skis

6. Studs

7. Wheels

8. Chassis

1

2

3

5

8

24

6

4

There are more than 225,000 miles (362,102 km) of snowmobile trails in North America. Placed end to end, they would almost reach the moon.

Snowmobile riders explore a remote area.

SNOWMOBILES IN ACTION

Most people use their snowmobiles for fun. They love the freedom of cruising through snowy forests or over snow-covered fields. Some people use their sleds for work. For example, park rangers and farmers use them to get to hard-to-reach places. Rescue workers use snowmobiles to reach people who need help on frozen lakes or snowy mountainsides.

Others enjoy racing snowmobiles. There are many different racing series and styles of racing. Cross-country races wind through natural terrain. Derby races are held on oval tracks built on frozen lakes. But the most popular kind of racing is snocross. This sport is based on motocross. Racers push their machines to the limit over a course of bumps, jumps, and sharp turns. Amsoil Championship Snocross is the top snocross racing series.

FAST FACT

One of the first derby races was held on a Wisconsin lake in 1964. Eighth grader Stan Hayes was the winner!

Snocross riders race at the 2009 Winter X Games.

Snowmobile freestyle became a popular event o the Winter X Games.

By the 2000s, riders were doing more than just racing. Snowmobile freestyle exploded in popularity. Riders thrilled fans by doing tricks off of big jumps. They did daring Superman jumps, backflips, and more. These riders push snowmobiles to new limits. The people who built the first snowmobiles probably never imagined what they can do today!

FAST FACT

The world's longest snowmobile race is the annual Iron Dog. Racers travel more than 2,000 miles (3,219 km) to the finish line.

GLOSSARY

body armor
A body-fitting piece of strong plastic and foam that snocross racers wear under their clothing.

carbon fiber
A very strong, lightweight material made of woven threads of carbon.

chassis
The main metal frame of a snowmobile.

cross-country
A type of race in which riders drive over natural terrain.

modify
To change a vehicle to make it more suitable for another purpose.

snocross
A type of race held on snow-covered courses with lots of turns and jumps.

stud
A metal spike that is attached to a snowmobile's track to give it better grip.

suspension system
The system of shock absorbers and springs that connects a snowmobile's chassis to its wheels.

terrain
The shape of natural land.

track
Flexible belts that fit over a snowmobile's wheels; the wheels spin the track, which grips the snow and allows the snowmobile to move.

FOR MORE INFORMATION

Books

Older, Jules. *Snowmobile: Bombardier's Dream Machine*. Watertown, MA: Charlesbridge, 2012.

Tieck, Sarah. *Snowmobiles*. Edina, MN: Abdo Publishing Co., 2010.

Websites

To learn more about Speed Machines, visit **booklinks.abdopublishing.com**. These links are routinely monitored and updated to provide the most current information available.

INDEX

ABOUT THE AUTHOR

Matt Scheff is a freelance author and lifelong motor sports fan living in Minnesota.